SALT LAKE CITY
THEN & NOW

SALT LAKE CITY THEN & NOW

KIRK HUFFAKER

THUNDER BAY
P·R·E·S·S

San Diego, California

Thunder Bay Press
An imprint of the Advantage Publishers Group
10350 Barnes Canyon Road, San Diego, CA 92121
www.thunderbaybooks.com

Produced by Salamander Books,
an imprint of Anova Books Ltd.,
10 Southcombe Street, London W14 0RA, U.K.

All notations of errors or omissions should be addressed to Thunder Bay Press,
Editorial Department, at the above address. All other correspondence (author
inquiries, permissions) concerning the content of this book should be addressed
to Salamander Books, 10 Southcombe Street, London W14 0RA, U.K.

ISBN-13: 978-1-59223-836-1
ISBN-10: 1-59223-836-X

Library of Congress Cataloging-in-Publication Data

Huffaker, Kirk.
  Salt Lake City then & now / Kirk Huffaker.
    p. cm.
  ISBN 978-1-59223-836-1
  1. Salt Lake City (Utah)--Pictorial works. 2. Salt Lake City (Utah)--History--
Pictorial works. I. Title. II. Title: Salt Lake City then and now.
  F834.S243H84 2007
  979.2'25803--dc22
                          2007040591

1 2 3 4 5 12 11 10 09 08

Printed in China.

ACKNOWLEDGMENTS
Thank you to Robin Pratt and Mike Eldredge for helping me get this project off the ground. The staff at the
Utah History Research Center at the Utah State Historical Society is held in my highest regards for all their
friendly assistance and professionalism, and I give special acclaim to my friend Alan Barnett for his guidance.
For their assistance with information, unique photographs, and drafts, I benefited from the help of Steve
Scott, Mike Davis, Anne Oliver, and Randy Dixon. Cathy Kim, you went above and beyond to help out.
A special dedication to Kristie Huffaker, and the Thompson and Huffaker families for their support.

PICTURE CREDITS
The publisher wishes to thank the following for kindly supplying the photographs that appear in this book:

"Then" photographs:
All "Then" photographs are courtesy of Utah State Historical Society, except for the following:
Church History Library, Salt Lake City for page 86; Special Collections Dept., J. Willard Marriott Library,
University of Utah for pages 70, 124, and 126.

"Now" photographs:
All "Now" photographs were taken by David Watts (© Anova Image Library), except for pages 97 and 143,
which were taken by Catherine Fegan-Kim.

INTRODUCTION

The Great Salt Lake, from which Salt Lake City derives its name, is the second-largest inland saltwater sea in the world. Approximately 16,000 years ago, in the Pleistocene epoch, a 20,000-square-mile body of water, which is now Lake Bonneville, extended west into Nevada, north into Idaho, and covered the Salt Lake Valley between the Oquirrh and Wasatch mountain ranges. The Great Salt Lake and its western desert counterpart, the Bonneville Salt Flats, are the glacial remains of Utah's last ice age.

The Fremont and Anasazi peoples, who hunted and farmed in the Salt Lake Valley, were the most populous tribes in Utah for 10,000 years. These early tribes were succeeded in the 1400s by the modern Ute and Shoshone groups, who lived a nomadic lifestyle, sharing the valley and trading with fur trappers as early as 1820.

Joseph Smith Jr. founded the Church of Jesus Christ of Latter-day Saints (commonly known as the LDS or Mormon Church) in 1830. Smith's followers relocated from New York to Ohio and Missouri, ultimately arriving in Illinois. From 1839 to 1846, the Mormon colony of Nauvoo, Illinois, grew and prospered until Smith and his brother Hyrum were murdered by a mob. The Mormons were driven out of Nauvoo at gunpoint.

Brigham Young headed the Mormon Church after Smith's demise and captained the caravan of pioneers that left Nauvoo in 1846 in search of a new, western home. However, the main trip west from Nebraska would have to wait until 1847. In the spring of that year, the first wagons and handcart companies set out on the Oregon and Mormon trails for the 1,300-mile trek across the Rocky and Wasatch mountains, enduring extremely harsh conditions.

Arriving in the Great Salt Lake Valley on July 24, 1847, the settlers uniquely laid out Salt Lake City according to Joseph Smith's plat of Zion, with 120-foot-wide streets and ten-acre blocks, creating a city unlike any in the East. Between 1847 and 1869, approximately 70,000 Mormons would come to Salt Lake City via the Mormon Trail.

In 1850, the U.S. Organic Act created the Utah Territory. Numerous major building projects were started in the center of Salt Lake City, including the Salt Lake Temple in 1853, Brigham Young's Beehive and Lion houses in 1854, and the Mormon Tabernacle in 1864.

The non-Mormon population began to arrive in 1862 when U.S. military troops established Camp Douglas to protect the overland mail route, but unofficially also to keep a watchful eye on the Mormons. At Promontory Summit, a hundred miles north of Salt Lake City, the first transcontinental railroad was joined in 1869. This event facilitated the early and rapid growth of Salt Lake City and Ogden as Utah's major rail destinations for many decades.

Utah's exposure to the first railroads opened the market to develop the mining industry in the 1870s. Discoveries of silver in Park City and copper in the Oquirrh Mountains bordering the Salt Lake Valley attracted new immigrant populations in the 1880s to Utah cities as a labor force, populating camps and towns such as Park City, Bingham, Brighton, and Alta.

Many prominent businessmen, politicians, and religious leaders had taken strides to assimilate Utah into the American mainstream. Culmination of these actions was taken by the fourth president of the LDS Church, Wilford Woodruff, when he issued his manifesto prohibiting further polygamous marriage, which largely cleared the way for Utah's statehood on January 4, 1896.

Statehood prompted Utah to boom with new ideas. The cultural community of the state grew in the arts and humanities, as well as with the establishment of social, political, and women's organizations. The pre–World War I years brought many new downtown building projects, including the Utah State Capitol, two railroad depots, Hotel Utah, and the Federal Building expansion. Samuel Newhouse began his mini Wall Street in Salt Lake City, erecting four buildings on Exchange Place.

Skiing evolved into a popular sport in the 1930s and led to the development of the first ski areas, including Alta and Snow Park (now Deer Valley). The downtown Broadway Shopping District had always been something to dress up for, but in the post–World War II heyday, it was a treat to visit local stores like Auerbach's and Keith–O'Brien.

The economics of downtown turned sour from the late 1950s through the early 1970s, which meant the demise of many iconic buildings as well as cultural districts such as Japan Town and Chinatown. By 1980, many businesses left for the suburban shopping malls, closed up, or moved to the ZCMI Center and Crossroads Mall at the north end of Main Street.

By the mid-1980s, business owners and patrons believed in downtown again. The concept of historic preservation utilized older buildings to attract people to new restaurants and unique office spaces.

To spur revitalization on the west side of downtown, artists invested in live-work spaces and sponsored gallery walks, and a new home was built for the National Basketball Association's Utah Jazz in the early 1990s. Around Salt Lake City's compact downtown, traditional neighborhoods benefited from city residents caught in the fever of renovation. With small shopping districts, parks, and schools, these areas feel more like distinct villages, making them a major strength of the urban fabric of the city.

By the late 1990s, the surge to move back downtown hit Salt Lake City and historic warehouse loft space was in high demand. The culture, nightlife, shopping, and shorter commute associated with living downtown were primary factors in attracting the new residents.

Winter recreation and skiing remain as popular as ever, thanks in part to Salt Lake City hosting the 2002 Winter Olympic Games. In 2006–2007, over 4 million visitors skied Utah's "Greatest Snow on Earth."

Though we have entered a new millennium, the pioneer ideal to create a city of permanence is still celebrated on July 24, Pioneer Day, the day the first Mormon pioneers entered the Salt Lake Valley. This ideal is also expressed through the quality of new structures, including the City Library and LDS Conference Center, stewardship of Salt Lake City landmarks such as historic Temple Square, and the surrounding neighborhoods.

Though Salt Lake City's shopping, working, and living patterns have changed, the unique streetscape and historic buildings that create its sense of place have not. With careful future planning, the plat of Zion and the landmarks built within it will remain for generations of residents and visitors to use and enjoy.

The development of the ten-acre Temple Square began with Brigham Young's siting of the Salt Lake Temple. A fifteen-foot wall surrounding the block became the first permanent structure when new arrivals in the city were given make-work projects as early as 1852. The Tabernacle (center) and Salt Lake Temple (right) were constructed on the grounds first, with work on the temple progressing over the course of forty years. The charming Assembly Hall of 1882 (left) is in no way second fiddle to the famous domed Tabernacle or the six-spired Salt Lake Temple. Obed Taylor designed this Gothic-style structure as a meeting hall for about 2,000 people using the cast-off granite from the temple. Temple Square was already a sanctuary within private walls in this 1909 photograph, with ornamental landscaping woven throughout a series of walking paths.

Temple Square is the heart of Salt Lake City. The street grid for the Salt Lake Valley originates from its adjacent streets. It is also Salt Lake City's spiritual heart, as it is the site most visited by tourists to the state of Utah as well as a gathering place for community events such as the annual Lights On celebration for Christmas. Since the Salt Lake Temple, Tabernacle, and Assembly Hall are at the center of the faith for the Church of Jesus Christ of Latter-day Saints, also known as the Mormon Church, the stewardship of these buildings has been exceptional. Among the landscaping throughout Temple Square, various fountains and sculptural monuments relating to Mormon historical events, such as the Seagull Monument and the Mormon Handcart statue, can be discovered.

Four days after entering the Salt Lake Valley, Brigham Young hiked Ensign Peak to locate the proper place for a temple. On April 6, 1853, a long construction process commenced when he laid the cornerstone of the temple foundation. Years stretched into decades as construction slowed or stopped for financial, political, and design reasons. Granite was quarried in Little Cottonwood Canyon, twenty miles southeast, and transported to the site by teams of oxen. As each block of granite weighed about three tons, a single wagonload required four days of travel to reach the temple site. The granite was later brought by railroad. Dedication of the temple took place on April 6, 1893, forty years after it was begun, presided by Wilford Woodruff, the fourth president of the LDS Church.

The Salt Lake Temple's six distinctive Gothic towers topped by finial spires and a statue of the angel Moroni are recognizable across the world as the centerpiece of the Mormon faith. It's hard to believe that the temple was estimated to have cost only $4 million by the time it was completed, most of it in donated time and labor. The amazing details of its construction can be seen at the base in its fifteen-foot-thick granite walls as well as in the details of the west side bas-relief sun, moon, and stars that represent the three degrees of Mormon heaven. The traditional and symbolic importance of the Salt Lake Temple has been carried through its spires into the design of other temples around the world.

The Salt Lake Mormon Tabernacle was built between 1864 and 1867 using the temple's west elevation axis as its center line. Architect William H. Folsom and bridge builder Henry Grow employed the ideas of architect Ithiel Town and used a lattice-truss arch system that is joined together by a dowel and wedge construction technique to create a clear span of 150 feet without center supports. Architect Truman O. Angell was employed in 1870 to design a gallery, which happened to remedy acoustic problems in the building when it was completed in 1875. The Tabernacle was considered an amazing achievement in both engineering and acoustics for its time. The Mormon Tabernacle Choir started from a small group organized to sing at a church conference on August 22, 1847. The choir broadcast their first "Music and the Spoken Word" program on network radio on July 15, 1929, from this building, and appeared on national television in the 1960s.

In 2005, the LDS Church closed the Tabernacle for renovation and the unique task of retrofitting the building to withstand an earthquake while upgrading its performance qualities. After twenty-three months, the Tabernacle reopened in March 2007 stronger than before. However, after several renovations over the years to the Tabernacle, the original capacity of 8,000 has been reduced to 3,456. Engineers who worked on the building believe it is one of the most ingenious systems ever built and commented on the good condition of the original leather straps that hold the building's truss system together. One can still hear a pin dropped at the pulpit from the back of the hall, 170 feet away. The Mormon Tabernacle Choir erupts in joyous voice every week in the Tabernacle, making it Utah's version of Old Faithful.

During Salt Lake City's first thirty years, Brigham Young's Lion and Beehive houses anchored the heart of the settlement. The design of both houses is credited to Truman O. Angell, Young's brother-in-law. Finished in 1855, Beehive House, on the right with the two-story porch, uniquely adapted Greek Revival and New England styles for the locally available adobe building materials. Beehive House served as Young's executive mansion while he was governor of the Utah Territory and president of the LDS Church. Lion House, on the left,

was completed in 1856 as a home for as many as twenty of Brigham Young's wives and dozens of their children at one time. The floor plan of the house was a model for polygamous living arrangements with a basement dining room, main floor sitting room and kitchen, and twenty children's bedrooms on the third floor, one under each gable. The floor plan reflected the need to balance space and standing among plural wives.

The restoration of Beehive House began in 1959, guided by original drawings, extensive archival investigation, on-site exploration of the physical structure's composition, and input from a committee that included Young's descendants. Beehive House was restored to function as a museum and, since it reopened for visitors in 1961, it has been one of the most popular tourist sites in Utah. The Lion House was restored to some extent in 1968, although its interior remains open to accommodating receptions and restaurant dining. The design of the Lion House represents perhaps the most visible way to still see how the nineteenth-century Mormon belief system of polygamy emerged in its architecture. In seeing the Beehive and Lion houses, one can begin to know Brigham Young. The houses are symbols of a man's faith, belief in a strong work ethic, and modest yet caring appointment to detail and fine craftsmanship.

Eagle Gate was built in 1859 as the formal entrance to Brigham Young's estate. The design for Eagle Gate is attributed to Hiram B. Clawson, though Ralph Ramsey carved the original eagle for the gate. Ramsey also did original woodwork in the Beehive and Lion houses, and became known as a prolific woodworker throughout the state. In 1882, State Street was opened as a thoroughfare from South Temple through the Eagle Gate. The original gate was twenty-two feet wide. In this photo from about 1885, one can see the nine-foot wall that surrounded Young's estate, supposedly to protect against Indians, and Beehive House in the background. Eagle Gate's function as a toll booth is an urban myth. However, wood cut at Young's sawmill was taken as the toll for using his property to go up City Creek Canyon. In its prominent location, the expansive wings of this eagle took on the symbolism of the unofficial gateway to the city.

A larger version of Eagle Gate was erected in 1891 to handle the increased traffic from streetcars and horse-drawn wagons and carriages. Joseph Don Carlos Young, son of Brigham Young, was the architect for the second Eagle Gate. In 1960, a truck knocked an arch of Eagle Gate from its pillar and the gate was deemed irreparable. Due to its symbolism, the LDS Church and the Utah State Road Commission determined that Eagle Gate should be rebuilt, and this was an opportune time to widen State Street. George Cannon Young, son of Joseph Don Carlos Young, designed the new Eagle Gate in a concept with the spirit and bold design of the flying buttresses, and Grant Fairbanks sculpted a new soaring eagle. Dedicated in 1963, the third Eagle Gate stands seventy-six feet wide, providing a stately entrance to the heart of the city by enframing the state capitol.

At the turn of the twentieth century, business and religious leaders set aside their differences to build something great that could promote Salt Lake City. In gleaming white terra-cotta rose the Hotel Utah, the "Grande Dame of Hotels." From its opening in 1911, the Hotel Utah was widely held as the finest accommodations in the city. Parkinson and Bergstrom of Los Angeles designed the $2 million, H-shaped structure with the prominent brick and plaster beehive as its apex. The Hotel Utah was able to ride out the economic lows of World War I and the Great Depression to enjoy tremendous success throughout the World War II era and into the 1970s. This photo from about 1950 shows the Hotel Utah during its heyday.

In 1988, the LDS Church began a five-year effort to adapt this landmark building for a new use. Located on one of the most prominent corners in downtown Salt Lake City, the extensive renovation left its magnificent lobby and ballrooms, as well as the rooftop restaurant, intact and open to the public. Many faithful Hotel Utah patrons were disappointed to see the building restored and reopened as office space for the Church of Jesus Christ of Latter-day Saints, but the decision preserved a major downtown landmark. The Joseph Smith Memorial Building opened in 1993 with all the elegance of the hotel era, from the ornamental Second Renaissance Revival architecture of the exterior to the restored interior spaces.

Latter-day Saints University was established as a religiously affiliated higher education institution in Salt Lake City so that Mormon Church members wouldn't have to travel to Provo to attend Brigham Young Academy. This concept was resoundly backed by the Mormon Church and the first classes were held in the Social Hall in 1886. Subsequently, the school expanded and moved to other locations, including Brigham Young's Eagle Gate Schoolhouse (1886), the Old Seventeenth Ward (1895–97), Templeton Building (1898–1900), and the Lion House. This photo of February 9, 1905, depicts the main quad of LDS University, including (from left to right) the Business College Building, Barratt Hall, and Brigham Young Memorial Building. By the time the campus was demolished in 1962, it had moved east and been renamed LDS Business College.

The life of the Gardo House was magnificent, but too short. In 1920, the house was sold for $100,000 to the LDS Church for a music school. However, the Federal Reserve Bank, an entity with growing national power at the time, offered to buy the house and replace it with a new building. The LDS Church tentatively announced plans to move the Gardo House but learned later that the $20,000 relocation cost was out of their budget range. Demolished in 1921, the prominent residence was replaced by the neoclassical Federal Reserve Bank in 1926. This structure was no longer needed when a new Federal Reserve Bank was built one block south in 1959 and it was demolished in 1984. The current Eagle Gate Plaza and Office Tower were constructed on the site in 1986, adjacent to the ZCMI Center, to provide office and retail space downtown.

One historian has called the Zions Cooperative Mercantile Institution, or ZCMI, America's first department store. Founded in 1868 as a commercial enterprise of the Mormon Church, the ZCMI promoted to Mormons the sale of merchandise that was made by Mormons. This proactive response to the transcontinental railroad ended up developing a regionwide system of local cooperatives. ZCMI sales totaled $1.25 million in its first year. In 1876, the cooperative's main store was built at the north end of Main Street with a prominent cast-iron facade of repeating arches designed by William H. Folsom and Obed Taylor. By 1910, the time of this photo, additions had been made to the right (in 1880) and left (in 1901) of the center block and the pediment was added to cap the building.

As an early example of historic preservation, the original ZCMI cast-iron and wood facade was cut off the building, disassembled, and reattached as a truncated version to the new ZCMI department store during the construction of the ZCMI Center in 1976. Today, this facade is regarded in historic preservation circles largely as "architectural sculpture" that is reminiscent of the former department store that graced downtown, rather than as a building. The ZCMI Center was slated for demolition in 2007 to make way for City Creek Center, a twenty-acre mixed-use development. Due to be completed in 2011, City Creek Center is managed by Property Reserve, Inc. (PRI), a real-estate development entity owned by the Church of Jesus Christ of Latter-day Saints, and will include a new Macy's department store on the site of the original ZCMI store. PRI plans to erect and reattach the original ZCMI facade to the new Macy's.

The Alta Club, shown here in 1905, was likely to be one of the few places in Salt Lake City at the time where members of two divergent communities could come together in acceptance. Unfortunately, deep divisions lay between Mormons and non-Mormons in the late nineteenth century, but the Alta Club and its membership of prominent Utah businessmen, largely involving those from the mining industry, gradually sought to change that. William Jennings—Utah's first millionaire, Salt Lake City's fifth mayor, and owner of the prominent Eagle Emporium on Main Street—was the first Mormon member. The Alta Club was founded in 1883 and built a permanent home in 1898 at South Temple and State Street. Membership expanded rapidly and an addition was built in 1910 to double the size of the club. The Packard Library, Salt Lake City's first public library, is seen to the right of the Alta Club, and a complex series of electric lines meet at the center pole of South Temple and State Street.

Looking past the traditional Second Renaissance Revival exterior will reveal that the Alta Club has continued its progressive leadership among clubs in Salt Lake City. Other clubs established and built grand buildings around the turn of the twentieth century—including the Elks Club, Odd Fellows Hall, and Commercial Club—but the Alta Club is the only one that survives in its historic location. In addition, its award-winning restoration in

2002 converted the vacant third floor into guest rooms, provided accessibility, and included a seismic upgrade. The University Club demolished its building to the left of the Alta Club and built the white skyscraper—with their club on top—in the 1970s. The former Packard Library from 1905 is to be restored as the retail store for O.C. Tanner. The Belvedere Apartments, beyond the library, were completed in 1920.

The Social Hall represents one of the most important early pioneer buildings in Salt Lake City, as it marks a strong tradition of community events and the arts. Brigham Young erected the hall in 1852 in order to have the arts better integrated into the community. Salt Lake Temple architect Truman O. Angell designed an attractive Greek Revival structure of adobe on a stone foundation and then covered it in plaster. Throughout its life, the hall has been used for theater, orchestra, dances, amusement, public gatherings, territorial legislature, and U.S. district courts. For major events, the main hall could hold 350 people and its popularity helped justify the construction of the Salt Lake Theatre, which took the Social Hall's place for large functions when it was completed. This photo was taken in 1920, near the end of the line for the Social Hall, which was demolished by January 1922. The Belvedere Apartments are to the left.

The ghost of the Social Hall is now represented in steel and glass over the original building site. While excavating for construction of an underground passageway beneath State Street, the original foundation of the Social Hall was discovered. An archaeological survey revealed the full size of the substructure, and other artifacts were uncovered. With the Social Hall's role in Salt Lake City's history as one of the first community gathering places, it was determined that the archaeological discovery would become part of the walkway. Many of the artifacts found during the excavation of the site were cleaned for the exhibit that is now part of the Social Hall Museum. The glass monument was dedicated in June 1992 and roughly represents the size and shape of the original building. Social Hall Avenue now leads from State Street to large parking garages and office buildings, which can be seen in the distance.

It is said that Utah theater had its beginning at the Salt Lake Theatre, which promoted the growth of amateur dramatic companies throughout Utah's settlements and attracted the best theater in the West to Salt Lake City. Construction of the 1,500-seat theater was funded by the LDS Church and completed in 1862. As the largest building in town, it dominated the city's streets, showing the importance of the arts in the community. Starting about 1915, when this photo was taken, motion pictures and vaudeville contributed to the theater's financial losses. The LDS Church made the decision in 1928 to demolish the building and sell the land to Mountain State Telephone Company. Demolition crews needed several months longer than originally planned, however, as the theater was so well constructed with large, red-pine timbers that the building proved to be a shining example of pioneer workmanship.

When LDS Church president Heber J. Grant announced that the Salt Lake Theatre was to be demolished, many saw it to be a violation of pioneer heritage. Despite heated public protest and alternatives promoted by the Daughters of Utah Pioneers, it was demolished in 1928. The theater's demolition began the historic preservation movement in Utah as the public began to recognize buildings of significance in the community and took action to save them. What rose on the site in 1939 was a two-story Art Deco structure. In 1947, an additional four stories were added as the demand for phone service increased. The former Mountain States Telephone and Telegraph Building, now owned by Qwest, is considered an architectural landmark in Utah and will remain on this corner as the City Creek Center project rises around it in the coming years. Behind it, the Key Bank Tower remains a major downtown office building, housing several law firms among other clients.

Salt Lake City's original vaudeville house, the Orpheum Theatre, was built in 1905. Carl Neuhausen's Second Renaissance Revival design gave the Orpheum its stage presence on State Street—he erected the twelve-foot-high statue of Venus directly above the entryway and placed dramatic sculpted faces along the street columns. Besides the theater, the building originally housed two stores, a boarding house, and a hotel. By 1918, the theater operated as a movie house under other names, including the Roxy, Lake,

and Lyric. In this photograph of the Lyric Theatre from 1947, one can see the fantastic signage that contributed to the street life. Angled parking was at a premium, as State Street's popular theater district intersected with the Broadway Shopping District two blocks south. Three more theaters can be seen on this side of State Street. The buildings to the south of the Lyric are representative of the high style of commercial architecture in Salt Lake City during this time.

In 1972, the LDS Church bought the theater and renovated it for live performances, christening it the Promised Valley Playhouse. In 1997, the building was closed as a safety precaution because it had not been seismically upgraded. The LDS Church did not perform this work, and during four years of negotiations, they could not reach an agreement to sell the building to Salt Lake County for use as a performing arts facility. In 2002, a 400-car parking garage was built on the site of the theater, connecting it to the front twenty feet of the building, which was spared from demolition. There are no theaters left on State Street today. In the distance, the Marriott City Center has risen at the corner, with Gallivan Plaza behind it.

William Paul designed the Eagle Emporium at Main Street and 100 South in 1864 for William Jennings's mercantile business. In this two-story sandstone building, ZCMI leased space and began operations in 1869, helping make Jennings Utah's first millionaire. In 1876, ZCMI moved to its own building one block north and soon afterward the Eagle Emporium (on the left-hand corner) was expanded to four stories, as seen here in this photo from 1918. At this time, the building was used by Utah First National Bank, which later merged with

Zions Bank. The McCornick Block (on the right) was completed in 1893, and at seven stories was taller than all other buildings downtown at the time. Dinwoodey's, whose painted name can just be seen on the left ("EY'S"), was a popular destination for many years for local furniture. Continuing straight down 100 South would take one into Japan Town. In the center of the street is a stoplight on a pole to control automobile traffic.

The Eagle Emporium's red sandstone was covered with white terra-cotta in 1916, as it was believed to be more fitting for a bank facade. In 1981, Zions Bank removed the top two stories of the building; it remains the current occupant. The Eagle Emporium is the oldest existing building downtown and the only building remaining from the period prior to the arrival of the railroad. Several of the smaller historic buildings at this intersection have been replaced over the years. Most noticeably, the Salt Palace Convention Center now serves as the terminus for 100 South. On the right side, construction of the Marriott Hotel fills a popular niche with the convention crowd. Dinwoodey's is now a Zions Bank office building and is covered with a blank facade that hides its original grandeur.

Architect Frederick Albert Hale's Commercial Block was a major landmark from the beginning, constructed in the rare Romanesque Revival style. Its architecture featured a prominent corner tower that extended along both major street facades into a multilayered frieze and cornice of decorative brickwork and corbelling. This site was adjacent to Commercial Street, later known as Regent Street, which also gave the building prominence as the entrance to a district widely known for its saloons and brothels from the 1870s to the 1930s. However, the Commercial Block had 125 offices as well as retail space on the ground floor. When Ross Beason & Co. bought the building in 1925, a year before this photo, its common name was changed to the Beason Building. The Walker Bank Building, seen to the left, was built in 1912 and was also considered a significant downtown building. At sixteen stories, the Walker Bank Building was the tallest building between St. Louis and the West Coast at the time.

Citing the need for more parking for the adjacent Walker Bank Building and in downtown Salt Lake City, the Beason Building was demolished in 1959 in front of 200 onlookers. A shift in the tenant mix in the Beason Block, from professional offices in 1935 to service industry and suppliers in 1958, may have brought lower rents and possibly helped justify replacement. Adjacent buildings on Regent Street were also demolished, including one on land that was once owned by Brigham Young but which had since been the location of a hotel that was frequented by Park City miners. The dynamics of the downtown area in this period were changing markedly, much to the detriment of historic buildings. The Walker Bank Parking Terrace was designed by the firm Skidmore, Owings & Merrill.

After arriving with the first pioneer company, Wilford Woodruff built the left section of the Valley House as his residence around 1851. This residence was across the corner from Temple Square, giving Woodruff a great location in the new settlement. The original house was likely a two-story, double-cell house with two rooms on each floor. By 1859, Woodruff, a farmer by nature, built a new farmhouse in the Big Fields area southeast of the city. In about 1873, the right section was constructed onto Woodruff's former house to create a hotel known as the Valley House. He also used the saltbox style (angled roofline) on his farmhouse, a style that is relatively rare in the rest of the state. The Valley House promoted itself as the city's only nonalcoholic hotel. The hotel finished its run in 1913—three years after this photo was taken—and was demolished in 1915.

Renovated in 1976 for the performing arts, the Capitol Theatre is home to touring Broadway shows as well as local companies such as Ballet West and the Ririe-Woodbury Dance Company. The Capitol Theatre's seating capacity of nearly 2,000 makes it one of the largest performing arts venues in the city. The Interstate Bank Building, now U.S. Bank, replaced the former buildings on the block in the 1980s. The Continental Bank Building was renovated in 1999 as the Salt Lake City Hotel Monaco. The steel arch remained in place until the early 1970s, when it was removed due to a new sign ordinance that targeted safety hazards; it was relocated to Trolley Square. The crossing signals in this photo serve as a faint reminder of the added activity the arch once brought to 200 South.

This photo was taken in 1910, shortly after the depot was completed. This station was Denver & Rio Grande Railroad owner George Gould's attempt to lure passengers away from Union Pacific with an impressive structure. It was built as the crown jewel of the railroad system at a cost of $750,000. Gould had been developing a transcontinental system to compete with Union Pacific ever since the golden spike was driven in at Promontory Summit in 1869, and he believed this ultramodern station with a grand public space and rich ornamentation would deliver the message that the Denver & Rio Grande was the better option. Due to fierce competition, Gould went broke shortly after the depot's completion and lost his railroad empire. The horse carriages seen here are waiting to pick up passengers and whisk them away to their destinations. One automobile can be seen in front of the doors on the right.

The Denver & Rio Grande had the choice to demolish the building in the early 1970s, when automobile and airline travel gave less justification for train travel and train stations. Maintenance of the depot had been neglected as costs skyrocketed. Instead, the building was sold in 1977 to the State of Utah. The state chose to renovate the depot as the new home for the Utah State Historical Society and a new restaurant, the Rio Grande Cafe. The

state even chose to maintain the vintage sign that the railroad installed on the roof. The Utah Arts Council joined the Historical Society as a tenant in 2005, using the Rio Gallery (the former passenger lobby) to promote Utah artists. The California Zephyr, the Rio Grande line's last luxury passenger train, serves as thematic decor in the Rio Grande Cafe, which has been housed in the north wing since the building reopened.

David and Joseph Peery knew how to build and run a hotel. With the construction of two new depots by the Denver & Rio Grande and Union Pacific railroads, the Peerys knew they should locate equidistant from both in order to have a favorable location for incoming passengers. The Peery Hotel was completed in 1910, at about the same time that the depots started accommodating travelers. This new E-shaped hotel provided natural light to all 156 rooms. The visually interesting features of the exterior can be seen in this photo from 1924, including the window detailing, quoins, and the cornice with paired brackets. Several other downtown hotels were built during this same period to take advantage of the increased railroad traffic and mining boom, including the Broadway, Garden, Great Western, Rio Grande, Semloh, and Shubrick hotels.

By 1952, the hotel had new ownership and changed its name to the Miles Hotel. The low point came during the 1970s, when it fell into disrepair and front windows were regularly boarded up. New owners renovated the hotel in 1985 and changed its name back to the Peery Hotel. Incompatible changes and years of neglect were reversed, and the number of rooms was reduced to seventy-eight so that private baths could be added. The Peery Hotel was upgraded again in 1999 with new ownership. The Peery is not only the last of the railroad-era hotels, it is one of the few historic hotels in Salt Lake City. To the left is the Rose Wagner Performing Arts Center, and to the right is the Shilo Inn.

In the 1860s, John T. McDonald sold saltwater taffy from his saddlebag while on horseback. His company went on to win forty-four gold medals for excellence and specialized in boxed chocolates and a chocolate drink intended to replace tea and coffee, which were considered "injurious" to Mormons. When the business transferred to his son, J. G. McDonald, it opened its three-story factory on 300 South (Broadway) in 1901. As the business grew more successful, the building expanded up and back, as can be seen from the varied style of windows. This January 1924 photo shows the building at its full size and is likely close to the company's peak, when they employed over 400 people. It had one of the two revered rooftop gardens in the city (the other being the Hotel Utah), with trees, flowers, and rare birds. The Garden Hotel, built in 1909, can just be seen to the left.

Downtown's nightlife and cultural attractions, unique shopping, and the lure of short commutes drove new residents to move to the area. By the late 1990s, renovations of former industrial buildings like the McDonald Chocolate Company helped attract a new and diverse set of residents. As one of the first loft conversion projects in the city in 1999, Broadway Lofts divided the building into fifty-eight units of varying sizes that retain the historic warehouse character with the addition of modern features. As part of the renovation, the previously removed fifth story was reconstructed as penthouse condominiums with garden patios. The Garden Hotel stopped operating in 1979 and is now Squatter's Brewpub, a popular destination for local microbrewed beer. To the right is a new building that houses the upscale Metropolitan restaurant.

In 1920, 300 South (Broadway) was bustling with window shoppers and sidewalk strollers. The Broadway Shopping District included all the best local stores—Auerbach's on the right, and the Paris and Keith–O'Brien on the left—as well as national stores like Kress, Sears, J.C. Penney, Woolworth's, and Walgreens, many of which could not be found in other Utah cities.

Eateries and coffee shops, like those in the Brooks Arcade (on the corner behind the Auerbach sign), were scattered along Broadway, providing shoppers with places to rest and eat. The sign over the intersection identified the fashionable retail district and helped in its promotion. Auerbach's later moved to the Keith–O'Brien Building, where it remained for about fifty years.

Several of Broadway's popular stores began to close in the late 1960s while local mainstays like Auerbach's, Keith–O'Brien, and the Paris remained as the shopping district's anchors into the 1970s, with Auerbach's holding out until 1979. Many of the buildings were demolished or remodeled beyond recognition, including the former Keith–O'Brien/Auerbach's Building, and since then the trend has been to grow "up." The Broadway Centre, in the right foreground, replaced the Centre Theatre, which replaced the former stone Auerbach's Building. The largest building is the Wells Fargo Center on the right. It was built in 1998 in the shape of an "A" for its original tenant, American Stores. The tallest building in the distance on the left is known as the J.C. Penney Building, which replaced the downtown Sears store, although J.C. Penney has only maintained office space in the building.

Two sites were considered for Utah's first federal building once statehood was granted in 1896: one across from Temple Square that was offered by the LDS Church, and another offered by the Walker brothers on South Main Street. After vocal opposition by non-Mormon leaders, the federal government chose to purchase the South Main Street location. James Knox Taylor, supervising architect of the U.S. Treasury, introduced the neoclassical style of architecture to Utah. As Taylor was an out-of-state architect, he may have been influenced by the City Beautiful movement in architecture and planning that originated at the 1893 World's Columbian Exposition in Chicago, which revived the country's interest in architecture and the use of classical styles. The facility, completed in 1905, served as the first major downtown post office and courthouse, relieving the Social Hall of some of its previous functions. The formal facade composition, symmetry, and Greek-ordered detailing are exhibited in this 1907 photo.

The Post Office and Federal Building was expanded in 1912 and again in 1932 but kept its classical proportions through both projects. The post office relocated to a new facility in west downtown in the mid-1970s, allowing expansion of the courts to occupy the entire space in the building, now the Frank E. Moss Federal Courthouse, named for the former U.S. senator from Utah. In recent years, the federal courts have again outgrown their space.

A new building is planned west of the courthouse as an annex to the complex to serve as the federal criminal courts. The Odd Fellows Building, to the right of the courthouse, will be moved across the street. Once that project has been completed, the historic Moss Courthouse will be renovated for continued use by the federal courts. The Little America Hotel can be seen to the left of the courthouse.

Boston & Newhouse Blocks
Salt Lake City

In 1907, mining kingpin Samuel Newhouse launched a significant building program to shift the center of the city four blocks south of Temple Square. Newhouse made millions in Colorado mining before the age of forty and spared no expense in life. Anchoring his building program were to be the Boston and Newhouse buildings, Utah's first skyscrapers. Henry Ives Cobb, a Chicago/New York architect, brought the elegance and prominence of other cities' architecture to Salt Lake City with the first buildings of Exchange Place in 1909. Seen here soon after construction, the buildings represented large columns with a base, shaft, and capital. The Boston Building (left) was named after Newhouse's Boston Consolidated Mine.

The Boston and Newhouse buildings are iconic structures in downtown Salt Lake City, representing Newhouse's beliefs in business competition, great architecture, good city planning, and personal indulgence. Though they may look like twins, subtle details tell them apart. Both buildings have office space on the upper floors and retail outlets at ground level. Unfortunately, Newhouse overextended himself beyond his mining profits and by 1914 could not fund his building projects sufficiently. Plans for another pair of buildings similar to the Boston and Newhouse at the opposite end of Exchange Place never came to fruition, nor did plans for a hotel and theater project within the block.

Samuel Newhouse obtained a major section of land at the non-Mormon south end of Main Street, to fulfill his dream of having a mini Wall Street in Salt Lake City. Newhouse belonged to prestigious clubs and had offices in New York, London, and Paris, and wanted to bring the advantages of those cities to Utah. By 1910, the date of this photo, the focal buildings of Exchange Place had been completed. The Commercial Club, on the left, was a luxurious predecessor to the chamber of commerce; members could meet for lunch or take a dip in the top-floor swimming pool. The Salt Lake Stock and Mining Exchange, with the columns on the right, was founded in 1888 to raise development capital for Utah's silver mines. In the 1950s, the exchange would be the center of the world during the uranium boom as the trading of uranium futures developed the mines of Moab, in southern Utah.

As the second major commercial district in Salt Lake City, Exchange Place was recognized as a national and local historic district in the mid-1970s. Its significance is tied to the progressive method of construction, steel frame and masonry, the integrity of the architecture, and the buildings as a reflection of Utah's mining wealth in the early twentieth century. In the 1980s, a public plaza closed Exchange Place to traffic and several parking garages were demolished. Today, the buildings of Exchange Place form a professional office environment with a unique sense of place that appeals to a wide variety of tenants. A few new art galleries, restaurants, and shops fill storefronts. The one constant that Newhouse ensured is that the impressive facade of the Federal Building will always serve as the visual terminus of Exchange Place.

The Great Depression hit Salt Lake City and Utah particularly hard. After 1925, no major buildings were constructed in downtown Salt Lake City for thirty years. The First Security Bank Building changed the face of downtown forever as the first International Style building as well as the first major construction project since the Great Depression. Built in 1955, First Security Bank was considered futuristic, and the design was truly pioneering. A steel skeleton was covered with Utah's first curtain wall of green glass and porcelain-coated steel panels in a colorful red, gray, and cream palette. First Security Bank president George S. Eccles believed it was a bold step to choose a modern architect, W. A. Sarmiento, to lead First Security Bank, the banking industry, and Salt Lake City into a new era of prosperity.

First Security Bank anticipated that their new building would become a prestigious address for office space and an anchor for the south end of Salt Lake's commercial business district. However, businesses chose to relocate to the suburbs or to east downtown when new options became more attractive than a downtown location. After a merger with Wells Fargo, the First Security Bank Building was sold to Wasatch Real Estate Partners, which put the building at risk until they committed to a $12 million renovation. Preservationists recognized that the building could evoke a modern, efficient, and historic image of the city once again if given the chance. The building, which has recently been renamed for one of its major tenants, serves as the headquarters for the Ken Garff Automotive Group.

By the time of this photo in 1914, the Walker Bank Building had only recently taken over the skyline as the tallest building in downtown from the Boston and Newhouse buildings. Main Street was the center of commercial activity in Salt Lake City. The Grand Hotel, built in 1910 by mining baron John Daly, is the five-story structure on the corner. Since Daly was influential in the non-Mormon business community downtown, building the Grand Hotel near Exchange Place was likely solicited by Samuel Newhouse. Due to the substantial efforts of Newhouse, South Main Street, as seen here, was a growing intersection of business, government, and social life in downtown Salt Lake City.

The most apparent change between 1920 and today is that all the small commercial buildings within the block immediately in front of the City and County Building have been demolished. A few new buildings have taken their place, but for many years the main function of this block has been a parking lot. The new buildings on Main Street and State Street have grown taller and obscure many of the original, smaller buildings that do remain in between. The state capitol can still be seen in the distance. The former Keith–O'Brien Building and Brooks Arcade, while still recognizable parts of the streetscape, have been modified so as to not be considered historic buildings any longer. The second-tallest building on the left, with the copper dome, is One Utah Center, which was designed by the Salt Lake City firm VCBO and completed in 1991.

After several years of discussion, the city and county agreed to build a new combined courts, jail, and public safety facility called the Metropolitan Hall of Justice on the original site of the Salt Lake City Jail. Harold K. Beecher served as the architect for the $9 million New Formalist–style complex that looks like a giant filing cabinet. Major issues delayed the opening of the complex for several years, including a tunnel cave-in and a programming mix-up that resulted in the need for additional work. A new city library, which was designed by the architectural firm Edwards & Daniels and treated as a separate project, was begun at the same time as the Metropolitan Hall of Justice and was completed first. The Hall of Justice (completed in 1967) and Main Library block were viewed as a testament to 1960s progress and exhibited some of the best architecture of the era.

In 1998, Salt Lake City voters approved an $84 million bond to build a new main library. The Metropolitan Hall of Justice had been determined to be insufficient for public safety needs and was demolished in 1999. Architect Moshe Safdie was the lead designer for the Salt Lake City Main Library, which opened in February 2003. The crescent wall forms an interior space known as the Urban Room and serves as an entry to the library and the library shops. Walking on the arch takes one to the rooftop garden and viewing area. A five-story atrium inside the glass wall is linked with the Children's Library, which encourages imaginative reading experiences. The open public plaza of Library Square creates a link with Washington Square and there is a comfortable, engaging dialogue of historic and modern architecture between the City and County Building and the Main Library.

Greek immigrants were recruited to Utah by padrones, or Greek labor agents, to work long hours in mining, railroad gangs, sheepherding, and as shopkeepers. Despite long working hours, social networks and religious organizations kept the old-world community alive with music and dancing. Salt Lake City was the center of the state's Greek community and its Greektown grew to a peak of over sixty businesses in 1910. As the Greeks became the largest ethnic labor force in the state, their first church was deemed inadequate and Holy Trinity Greek Orthodox Church was constructed in 1924 to replace it. Architect N. A. Dokas of Chicago and the Salt Lake City firm of Pope & Burton collaborated on a design that was traditional Byzantine Revival in the form of a cross, with a large central gold dome where the transept crosses the main section.

The physical reminders of Greektown are left to a few commercial buildings on 200 South. However, Holy Trinity remains as a shining example of the faith and devotion of the Greek Orthodox community in Salt Lake City today. A restoration of Holy Trinity was completed in 2006. On the exterior, masonry work has restored the intricate alternating horizontal and vertical brick patterns and elaborate capitals. Two copper-domed bell towers, the tile roof, and the blue and gold tiles that frame the arcaded entryway are architectural features that stand out after the restoration. The walls and the ceiling on the interior are decorated with murals that depict lessons of faith bringing heaven to earth. The Hellenic Cultural Center for the church is located to its left. As a part of the city's growing west side, the diversity of culture that Holy Trinity Greek Orthodox Church represents will be important to maintain.

Japan Town became a recognized place around 1907 when the Japanese community was centered on several blocks of 100 South on the near west side of downtown. Much of the focus of the Japanese culture in the community was in the churches, including the Japanese Church of Christ, seen in this photo from 1923, and the Buddhist Temple. Both were located in the heart of Japan Town among the residences, noodle houses, bathhouses, fish markets,

tofu makers, and the Japanese language school. Walter Ware designed the modest Tudor Revival–influenced Japanese Church of Christ, which was constructed in 1923. The Japanese population of Utah tripled in 1946 when many of those who had been living at the Topaz Internment Camp near Delta, Utah, and on the West Coast relocated to Salt Lake City.

In 1969, expansion of the Salt Palace Convention Center—the walls of which can be seen behind the church—demolished the heart of Japan Town, except for the Japanese Church of Christ and the Buddhist Temple. These houses of worship continue to serve as the center of the traditional Japanese community in Utah with events such as the Obon Festival (a Buddhist festival of dancing and music to honor the dead) being held annually between the buildings. The convention center provided the space to attract new tourists to Utah, but during the late 1960s, in the days of urban renewal, there was not much discussion about demolishing the physical history of a culture. Today, there are renewed discussions about the revitalization of Japan Town. The first steps have been taken with the naming of 100 South as Japan Town Street and the planting of a traditional Japanese garden adjacent to the Japanese Church of Christ for the public's enjoyment.

Emmanuel Kahn was one of the first Jewish settlers in Utah when he arrived in 1867. He and George Bodenburg opened a small grocery business that operated under the name Kahn Brothers. Their business was highly successful and grew to include several buildings on the near west side of downtown. Kahn Brothers opened the buildings between 1901 and 1923, all conveniently close to the railroad lines along 400 West. This photo was taken soon after the Kahn Brothers warehouse on 400 West was built and occupied in 1913. Unlike many warehouses in the area, the facade of the Kahn warehouse is adorned with Classical Revival features, including pilasters, medallions on the frieze, and a cornice of dentils. The fence in the foreground belongs to the Union Pacific Depot.

Construction of a new sports arena near downtown began in November 1990 and was completed in an amazing fifteen months in order to be ready for the Utah Jazz basketball season in 1991. The building was designed by the Salt Lake City architectural firm FFKR and was subsidized in part by the Salt Lake City Redevelopment Agency to spur revitalization on the west side of the city. Built on the site of the demolished Kahn Brothers warehouse, the arena's location was questioned by many, but today parking is at a premium and riding the TRAX mass transit system is encouraged to get to this popular area of town. Known for years as the Delta Center, the recently renamed Energy Solutions Arena holds 20,500 at its capacity for concerts, a variety of indoor sporting events, and remains the home of the Utah Jazz.

Shown here in 1902, the west side of Salt Lake City's downtown was evolving from a quiet residential neighborhood to an industrial and warehousing district complete with railroad spurs to every building. The Henderson Block, the prominent sandstone and brick building on the right, was completed in 1899. Wilber S. Henderson's wholesale grocery business grew during the period of railroad expansion in Salt Lake City to become one of the largest grocers in the state and Henderson used this location as his headquarters. Typical for many of Salt Lake City's wide streets at the turn of the twentieth century, the streetcar lines were being laid down the middle of the street, leaving enough room in the center for the electrical poles.

Warehouses and railroad spurs continued to be built in the neighborhood through the 1930s. This area is commonly known today as Gateway. In the late 1970s, it was nominated to the National Register of Historic Places as the Warehouse Historic District. In 1978, a planning report proposed the revitalization of a sixty-one-block area in this neighborhood. This groundbreaking planning report slowly converted skeptics into the first developers of warehouses for new businesses, housing, and restaurants.

The Henderson Block looks as timeless today as it did back then thanks to solid design, construction, and management. Beyond the Henderson Block is the Artspace project in the California Tire & Rubber Building. The first building on the left is the Dakota Lofts, which in 1998 was one of the first market-rate warehouse loft conversion projects downtown. In the distance on the left are grocery warehouse buildings that are being renovated for residential use.

The signing of the Pacific Railway Act by President Abraham Lincoln during the Civil War cleared the path for a northern transcontinental railroad route rather than the southern route that had been under consideration. The route was planned through Utah but a little farther from Salt Lake City than locals desired. However, Brigham Young ensured that a rail line would be built to Salt Lake City as soon as possible. At a cost of $300,000, Union Pacific's new depot for that line served its subsidiaries of the Utah Southern, Utah Central, and San Pedro, Los Angeles, and Salt Lake railroads. As this photo depicts in 1910, the new depot was a grand structure at the terminus of South Temple that uniquely blended Victorian, Classical, and Second Empire architecture. The public waiting room's vaulted ceiling has painted murals at either end, depicting the driving of the golden spike and the pioneers entering the valley.

Salt Lake City's Railroad Consolidation Plan of 1996 proposed combining underutilized rail lines behind the Union Pacific Depot, allowing for the shortening of highway viaducts and the opening of hundreds of new acres near downtown to development. The Gateway Lifestyle Center was completed in 2001 with the Union Pacific Depot as its centerpiece. The depot was renovated for tenants in both wings and the public waiting room has been converted to a reception space and lobby for the lifestyle center.

New architecture that surrounds the historic depot plays off its eclectic styles in the brick, roofline, and window patterns, as seen in the tower to the left. The lifestyle center features 105 stores and restaurants, 152 residences, and the Olympic Legacy Plaza featuring the "dancing waters" of the Olympic Snowflake Fountain. New TRAX light rail streetcar lines are being added in front of the depot on 400 West to extend the existing system to the Intermodal Hub.

The Utah State Fair is one of the state's oldest traditions, dating back to the 1850s. Since then, the fair has moved several times, including a stint during the 1880s when it was held southeast of downtown on Tenth Ward Square, where Trolley Square now stands. The state legislature moved the event to sixty-four acres on the banks of the Jordan River in 1902. The design for the Utah State Fairpark included a variety of buildings at prominent locations around a promenade. These buildings were all constructed during the early 1900s, including many by renowned local architects. The Mining and Manufacturing Building, the large building on the left, was designed by the architectural firm Ware & Treganza in 1905, and was the second major building constructed at the Fairpark. Seen here in 1909 from the promenade, the Mining and Manufacturing Building has historically been the most important building of the fair because of its location and size.

Agriculture and ranching are a way of life in Utah but are increasingly rare near Salt Lake City. While the annual Utah State Fair has been faced with the challenge of changing lifestyles, the state fair remains at the Fairpark. Thirteen of the original buildings are listed on the National Register of Historic Places and continue to be actively used in the Utah State Fair as well as for community events throughout the year. The Mining and Manufacturing Building was so severely deteriorated that it was condemned by the state and scheduled for demolition by 1985. A spirited effort was headed by the Fairpark to save its grandest building. In 1989, after a $12 million renovation, it reopened as the Grand Building. The Heritage Building, built around 1905, which is seen to the right of the Grand Building in the archival image, was traditionally known as the Floriculture Building. At the far right is the rustic Fish and Game Building designed by Pope & Burton architects in 1911.

The World's Columbian Exposition of 1893 in Chicago had a profound effect on America, but none perhaps larger than in the area of city planning and architecture. Designed by one of the deans of Utah architecture, Richard K. A. Kletting, the Salt Palace was said to be not unlike the Administration Building at the 1893 World's Fair. In addition, the complex around the Salt Palace was to be arranged in a parklike setting with a pond, Lombardy poplars, walks, and a Midway Plaisance with daily amusements, all of which were similar to those at the World's Fair. However, the Salt Palace was designed to promote the mineral, so salt crystals were affixed to the building for embellishment, allowing it to gleam by day and reflect 900 electric lights by night. Built in 1899 by a coalition of Salt Lake City businessmen, the Salt Palace served as an amazing dance hall, theater, and exhibition hall.

The Salt Palace burned down on August 28, 1910, and was never rebuilt. The surrounding amusement park continued to operate under the Salt Palace name and then later as Majestic Park. It was never the same, even with an early roller coaster and a saucer-shaped bicycle track that was reputedly the fastest in the country, as many world records were established on it. Although it stood for just eleven years, the Salt Palace is fondly remembered in Utah history as one of the greatest architectural structures that the city has ever seen. Today, an automobile dealership and hotel occupy a portion of the site. The original design of the site, with its grove of trees and walkway leading to the Salt Palace, can still be seen in the similar balance of an archway, street, and parking lot lights that now lead to the car dealership. The Salt Palace name lived on in the first professional sports arena and currently for the downtown convention center.

Ashton & Jenkins advertised their services as "developers of subdivisions for classy homes." Their contracting and development business started in 1902. In their other promotions, they advertised houses for "the city's progressive young men" and as places where one could "live next to nature." In this 1908 photo, workers are constructing houses at the Ashton & Jenkins subdivision on Conway Court, about three blocks south of the City and County Building. The subdivision consisted mainly of small bungalow-style homes in a range of materials, including wood shingles and brick. Their different forms dictated the size of the house, the degree to which these materials were used, and therefore the cost of the house.

Ashton & Jenkins helped establish Salt Lake City's reputation for having more bungalows than any other city west of Chicago. Wood had been in short supply since the pioneers arrived in 1847 and home buyers preferred brick construction, so the brick bungalow seemed like a natural fit for a growing city at the turn of the twentieth century. The subdivisions that Ashton & Jenkins built are highly desirable neighborhoods in Salt Lake City today.

The diversity of styles and high quality of housing in their subdivisions, such as Liberty Heights (1905), Fifth East Park Addition (1915), Gilmer Park (1921), and Country Club Acres (1930), have contributed to their popularity. Aside from a few uses of aluminum siding, Conway Court looks much the same as it did in 1908.

Indian hunters probably used Ensign Peak as a vantage point to scout for prey. However, the peak's modern significance is held in the geographical location of the Salt Lake Temple. While in Nauvoo, Illinois, Brigham Young had a vision that Joseph Smith, founder of the Mormon Church, showed him the peak and said, "Build under the point where the colors fall and you will prosper and have peace." Brigham Young was looking for this peak when he entered the Salt Lake Valley from the mouth of Emigration Canyon on July 24, 1847. Ensign Peak was named by Young after he climbed to the summit to survey the valley below and locate the proper place to build a temple. In this 1890 photo, the Salt Lake Temple is in the midst of construction, although the Tabernacle's roof is visibly complete. The wide expanse in the foreground is Arsenal Hill, the eventual building ground for the state capitol.

Ensign Peak is located at the northern end of Salt Lake City at an elevation 1,080 feet above the valley floor. Prior to the completion of the temple, religious ordinances were performed on Ensign Peak by the pioneer settlers as it became a symbolic gathering site. Ensign Peak has long been enjoyed for the spectacular panoramic view from its summit. Sunset is one of the best times to be on Ensign Peak. From the Utah State Capitol, State Street runs directly south for almost twenty miles, nearly the full length of the valley. Residential neighborhoods have grown around the state capitol into the foothills to the full extent that is permitted by the zoning code due to the steepness of slopes and allowances to protect the foothills. A nature park at the base of the Ensign Peak trail tells the historic story of the peak's symbolism through a series of plaques.

Architect Richard K. A. Kletting's last major commission, the Utah State Capitol, was perhaps his most accomplished work. His purely classical design won a competition among ten entries in 1912. The design and construction of the Utah State Capitol was delayed from statehood in 1896 due to the economic depression of the 1890s and a conflict between Mormons and non-Mormons regarding its planning. Kletting's capitol design was the only one that included a colonnade of Corinthian columns on three sides, as can be seen in this 1922 photo, and called for granite quarried from Little Cottonwood Canyon, like many other prominent Utah buildings. While Utah's capitol is reflective of the U.S. Capitol, its construction ultimately showed cooperation between once disparate factions and, in its choices, the state's desire to be accepted as a part of the United States.

The land for a state capitol was given to the Utah Territory by Salt Lake City in 1888 for the express purpose of constructing a state capitol building. Today, restoration of the Utah State Capitol is near completion. Similar to the City and County Building, the state capitol has been placed on 256 rubber base isolators to lessen risk during an earthquake. In addition, all the most prominent historic features and finishes have been restored, such as the Works Progress Administration–era murals that depict key moments in Utah's early history and the 165-foot-high rotunda with its 6,000-pound chandelier, which is suspended from a 7,000-pound chain. The original landscaping plan for the grounds will also be realized, incorporating an oval walkway that includes a stop at the Mormon Battalion Monument in the right foreground.

The area around City Creek that used to be owned by Brigham Young was set aside by Salt Lake City for use as a park in 1902. A stable and shed had been constructed here in about 1890 for contractor Patrick J. Moran. As it was located directly across from the city's water intake structure on City Creek, the city's water department used the building as its stable, barn, toolshed, and blacksmith shop. The city dedicated Memory Grove Park in 1924 as a place for veterans' activities and leased the building to the Service Star Legion. Salt Lake City architects Hyrum Pope and Harold Burton designed a new facade with a Georgian flair and the building was renamed Memorial House. The tall gray granite shaft, seen here about 1935, was dedicated in 1927 and erected by the 145th Field Artillery. Memory Grove Park is the beginning of City Creek Canyon. The state capitol can be seen above Memorial House.

After the Service Star Legion's lease ran out in 1984, Memorial House stood vacant for ten years. The Utah Heritage Foundation raised funds to renovate the building and in July 1994 the foundation opened the doors of Memorial House as its offices and an events center. On August 11, 1999, an F2 tornado traveled through downtown and into Memory Grove Park. The event resulted in the destruction of 478 mature trees. No buildings or monuments in the park were damaged, but the character of the park was changed forever. A steering committee for park planning and reconstruction was formed by Mayor Deedee Corradini and the path was laid for a new Memory Grove. Thousands of volunteers and several partners were part of an award-winning effort to restore the park with new trees, lighting, and native plants.

In 1776, the Dominguez-Escalante expedition was the first recorded crossing made by Europeans into Utah and began the long Catholic presence in the state. Utah's first Catholic church in Salt Lake City was consecrated in 1871. Construction of St. Mary's Cathedral started in 1899 following the design of architect Carl Neuhausen. Mining magnate Thomas Kearns and several other prominent Catholic residents of the city donated to the Pious Fund for the completion of the $300,000 building. With a gray Kyune sandstone exterior and an intricately detailed interior—which included twelve windows produced by the House of Littler of the Royal Bavarian Institute of Munich, Germany—the new cathedral took ten years to complete. Neuhausen died in 1907, and never got to see the finished church.

In the 1920s, St. Mary's Cathedral was renamed the Cathedral of the Madeleine. The picturesque religious structure helps form the backbone of South Temple and is one of Utah's architectural treasures. The Romanesque and Gothic exterior, which was restored in the late 1970s, displays some of the few gargoyles in Salt Lake City. A seismic upgrade was completed along with a meticulous interior restoration in 1993 that repaired stained glass windows, canvas wallpapers, murals, painted plaster, and cracked woodwork and carvings. From top to bottom, the project exemplifies quality restoration and dedication to both the symbolic and functional value of one of Utah's foremost historic structures. It received a National Honor Award in 1994 from the National Trust for Historic Preservation.

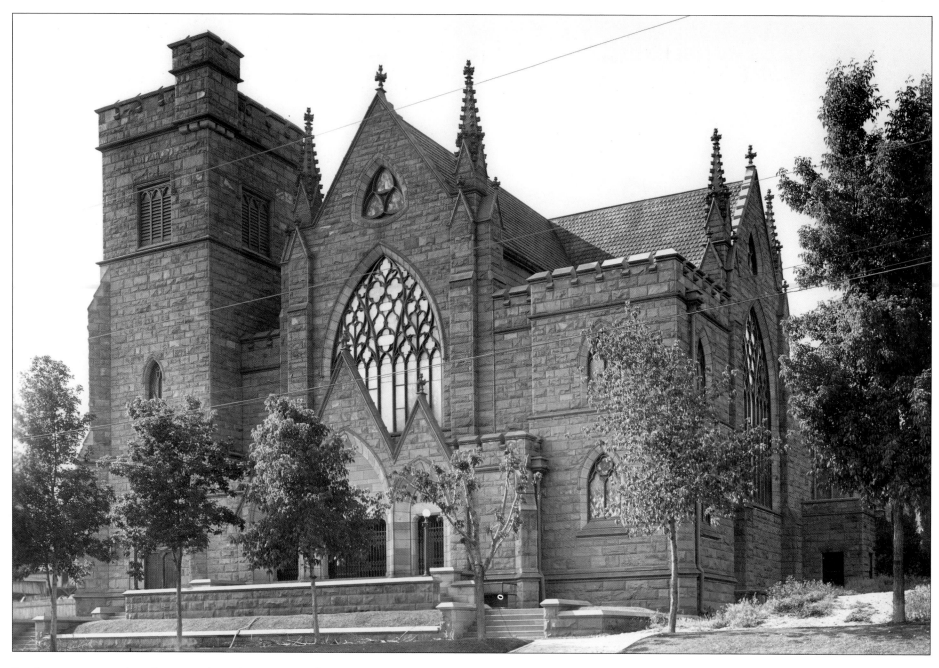

Presbyterians moved to the area when the mining industry grew, and others came as soldiers at Fort Douglas. In October 1871, Reverend Josiah Welch came to Utah to establish a Presbyterian congregation. The first locations included a livery stable hayloft and a building referred to as the skating rink. In 1901, four architects were invited to submit design proposals for a new church. After a year of deliberation, the congregation chose the design of Walter Ware. Ware's design was a blend of Gothic Revival and English styles, which he had researched by going to England. The eye-catching red sandstone was quarried in nearby Red Butte Canyon to the east and the stained glass windows were produced in Minneapolis. The building was dedicated in 1906, about a year before this photo was taken.

The congregation of First Presbyterian Church recognizes their strong bond with the past through their place of worship. One of the primary reasons may be the wonderful sanctuary that is a feast for the senses, blending light and color, aroma and texture. The centennial restoration was completed in 2003 with the theme "Everything Old Is New Again." In this eighteen-month project, the organ was renovated, stained glass was meticulously removed piece by piece and restored, and several sections of the building—including the sanctuary—were brought up to modern building codes for historic buildings. First Presbyterian Church has always been a masterpiece of church architecture, but this restoration provided a renewed sense of purpose and inspiration. The building seen to the left is associated with the Cathedral of the Madeleine.

In a true rags-to-riches story, Thomas Kearns left home at the age of seventeen and labored in the mines. He staked a mining claim that made him a millionaire at twenty-eight. Kearns became Utah's U.S. senator and copublisher of the *Salt Lake Tribune*. Using the finest craftsmen and materials available, the Kearns Mansion was created to be on par with any other châteauesque residence back East. Carl Neuhausen designed the mansion, which was completed in 1902. The Kearns had a hand-set, two-lane bowling alley in the basement. However, the two South American monkeys they kept would throw lightbulbs on the alleys and rip insulation from the pipes. The smaller building to the right, with a plaster horse over the entry door, is the carriage house. The State of Utah received the mansion as a donation from Jennie Kearns in 1937 for use as the state's first official governor's residence.

The Kearns Mansion, home of Utah's governor, remains arguably the finest mansion on South Temple. In history, it represents the important role of mining in Utah's development, and there were few other structures built in Utah to match the Kearns Mansion's extravagance. Demolition has taken away many of the other magnificent residences on South Temple, but Jennie Kearns's gift has saved one of the best on a street that continues to change with development pressure. Tragically, a December 1993 fire ignited by the traditional Christmas tree burned much of the grand front entry, staircase, and nearby areas in the mansion. The State of Utah went to extreme lengths in the restoration process, hiring the best restorers and making numerous structural improvements. When the Kearns Mansion reopened for public tours in the summer of 1996, thousands lined up to see the mansion restored to its 1902 appearance.

In 1890, the first public school system in Salt Lake City was established. Previously, education had largely fallen under the religious control of various faiths. A wealth of new buildings were constructed to serve the new school district, including the Oquirrh School in 1894, designed by Richard K. A. Kletting. *Oquirrh* means "shining mountains" or "mountains to the west" in the Piute Indian language. This 1903 photo shows the completed building of fifteen classrooms and a library, which cost the school district a total of $57,000. The board of education toured the building upon its completion and reported back that they believed they got their money's worth.

Declining enrollment in the commercial area of the city caused the closure of the Oquirrh School in 1965. The building had been condemned by the city and was in danger of being demolished. Instead, it became one of the city's first historic preservation success stories, as it was sold by the school district in 1973 and renovated for use as offices. Life for the Oquirrh School is about to come full circle, as the Children's Center has purchased the building. Their plans are to return children to the school building and ensure that the building's historic character remains intact. Sustainable building, or "green," principles are to be applied in its renovation. Depopulation of Central City has become a blessing in disguise, as all the other schools built between 1890 and 1930 have been demolished except for the Oquirrh School, which is once again a prominent school in the area.

This photograph from about 1945 was likely taken from Block U (above the location of the University of Utah) looking back at the valley. President's Circle at the University of Utah is in the center. The buildings of the university remain in their original condition from the time they were constructed. Along the Wasatch Mountains, the tall center peak is Mt. Olympus, which rises 9,026 feet above sea level. Between the university and the mountains, open fields exist along with some neighborhoods. As one can see from this photo, new subdivisions are being developed intermittently, with either new lots or new houses being built in the open areas. Development in the Olympus Cove area appears not to have started by this time.

Many of the buildings of President's Circle have been obscured by the University Hospital complex in the foreground. The University of Utah Hospital system has experienced tremendous growth since 1945, serving the region with several specialties. Mt. Olympus remains a favorite day hike for many in Salt Lake City, rising 4,200 feet above the valley floor for a spectacular view back to the Salt Lake Valley. The East Bench neighborhoods that are seen in this photograph—St. Mary's, Bonneville, Millcreek, Olympus Cove—are generally considered to be built out. These neighborhoods are faced with the demanding challenge of context-sensitive design or compatible infill development for new houses and large additions.

In the midst of the Civil War, soldiers were sent to Utah to protect the overland mail route. Arriving in October 1862, they established Camp Douglas, which later became the fort. In an unofficial capacity, the soldiers kept a watchful eye on the Mormons and prospected for potential mining sites in the mountains. The post headquarters was built in 1875 during a period of permanence at Fort Douglas where early buildings that were constructed of log or adobe began to be rebuilt more solidly in wood and stone. The majority of new buildings, such as the post headquarters, were built in the Gothic Revival style, as seen here in 1911. These off-duty soldiers are waiting for a ride into downtown to take advantage of their leave. During World War II, the building was used as the Officers' Club, a function that it continued until 1991, when the property was transferred from the U.S. Army to the University of Utah.

Fort Douglas is one of the most distinctive functioning historic sites in Utah. The military parade grounds, just beyond the Officers' Club, was once home to daily marching, military band practice, and field drills. Today it's a sports field and hangout for university students. The distinctive Gothic Revival architecture remains overwhelmingly intact and is being preserved by the University of Utah. In 2001, the Officers' Club underwent a $2 million renovation so that it could serve as a multiuse conference center. The Officers' Club is at the center of university life today, located at the crossroads of a walking path and streets, taking students to campus and student housing.

Brigham Young foresaw the need for a major university in Zion and founded the University of Deseret in 1850. In 1894, land was granted by Congress to the university on the East Bench near Fort Douglas for construction of a new campus, and the name was changed to the University of Utah. Classes opened on the new campus on October 1, 1900, with 400 students. These two buildings were among the first to be built; they were completed in 1901 and this photograph was taken shortly afterward. Designed by Richard K. A. Kletting, the highly decorative brick and sandstone buildings were located prominently on the East Bench above the city, and situated specifically around a central, west-facing oval drive. The Block U, seen here between the buildings, was first outlined in lime on the foothills and later filled in with concrete as an outward symbol of the university.

By 1914, eight buildings were completed around the oval; this composed the main campus of the University of Utah for several decades. These eight buildings served as the basis for ceremonies held during the 1970s to dedicate each one for a past president of the University of Deseret or University of Utah. With eight buildings around the oval, the naming of President's Circle was thus formally recognized. Between 1951 and 1975, the Cowles (Liberal Arts/Library) Building, to the right, was used by the Math Department, and from 1975 to the present the Communications Department has been the primary occupant. The Widtsoe (Physical Science) Building, to the left, is fully occupied by the Math Department. Both buildings' interiors have been substantially renovated by the State of Utah, with the exterior remaining wholly intact aside from the new addition to the north of the Cowles Building.

The Charleston Apartments were built in 1950 on one of the most prominent East Bench sites overlooking downtown. Salt Lake City architect Slack Winburn was selected for the Charleston because he had extensive experience designing other major apartment buildings, such as the Mayflower (1927) and University Gardens (1947). His design for the Charleston Apartments recalled the influence of fine Art Deco and Art Moderne structures of Miami Beach in massing, color, and style. However, it was one of the few substantial buildings in Salt Lake City that displayed period architectural features such as accentuated blocks of massing, meeting corner windows, and multidivision windows. Vertical scoring was used to create striated panels between windows, and deeply cut horizontal belt courses were employed to show division in the top and bottom sections of the building.

As times change, so do neighborhoods. In the 1960s, one could buy leather clothes, incense, and pottery at 9th & 9th. Popular stores here in the 1970s sold water beds. However, during the 1980s the construction of megatheaters made the operation of single-screen theaters like the Tower difficult, and it went out of business in 1988. A successful effort to save the Tower began in 1990. The Tower Theatre, the oldest operating theater in the Salt Lake

Valley, remains a vital element of the 9th & 9th neighborhood as a part of the Salt Lake Film Center, which promotes independent films, operates another theater location in downtown Salt Lake City, and occasionally uses the Tower as a venue for the Sundance Film Festival. Unlike most locations in the city, 9th & 9th is a multidimensional commercial district of restaurants, cafés, and retail stores surrounded by a residential neighborhood.

The innovations developed in millwright Frederick Kesler's twenty-nine mills profoundly influenced the success of Utah's pioneer settlements. Isaac Chase, a pioneer who emigrated from New York via Nauvoo, Illinois, built a grist mill on Emigration Creek between 1852 and 1854 with his partner Brigham Young. They used an experimental horizontal wheel but it was inefficient and broke often. Kesler was brought in and persuaded Chase and Young to redesign the mill in order to use the proven vertical wheel to generate power, which worked with much more efficiency. The Chase Mill shut down in 1879. Fortunately, Salt Lake City bought the Chase Farm and Mill in 1881 for the purpose of establishing a public park. The mill was a destination for Sunday drives in Liberty Park by 1930, the date of this photo, whether by car or by carriage. Notice the intricately woven, rustic wood fence, which was a signature element of Liberty Park at the time.

When the mill was threatened with demolition in 1898, a member of the Chase family persuaded the city not to demolish it. Instead, the Daughters of Utah Pioneers renovated the mill with private funds and used it for a museum through the 1950s. Today, the Chase Mill and Chase House are just a short walk apart and both have been excellently restored. The Chase Mill serves as an education and meeting center for the public and for the nonprofit organization Tracy Aviary, Utah's second-largest zoological society.

The basement is a teaching lab for students and the first floor of the building has exhibits about conservation. The upper floor holds a meeting space and library. The recent $1.3 million renovation included sustainable building principles as well as historic renovation of the original adobe building. The clerestory monitor roof can still be seen clearly—a signature characteristic of Kesler's mill architecture in Utah.

The Tenth Ward Square, former site of the state fair, became home to the Utah Light and Railway Company in 1907 after a major streetcar company merger. The distinctive Mission-style trolley barns were built on the site in 1908. The main building, seen here in 1915, stored and serviced streetcars at day's end. Maintenance services for the trolleys were conducted in the other four buildings of the complex, which were also used to store items for the citywide system of rails, electrical lines, and mechanical equipment. This facility kept the streetcars running in all types of weather. The main building had 208 skylights to provide natural light and used illuminated pits to allow streetcars to be inspected at night. Three buildings of the complex were built of brick around steel framework. Each square symbol within the arches displays the UL&R logo.

As the automobile became a necessity for every family, the streetcar fell out of favor. Though the trolley made a symbolic last run on May 31, 1941, the United States' entrance into World War II put the trolleys back on the tracks for another five years in an effort to conserve gasoline and materials. The barns remained vacant until they were renovated and reopened as a shopping center, Trolley Square, in 1972. As one of the earliest adaptive-use projects in

Utah and the United States, innovative architects and developers showed how capitalizing on unique architecture could result in profitable business. It was a bold step in uncharted waters for the time, but the public fell in love with the concept. The ninety-seven-foot-high, 50,000-gallon water tower that served the early fire sprinkler system for the buildings has become an iconic sign.

The Salt Lake Collegiate Institute was founded in 1875 when Presbyterian Church officials determined that it was time to establish a Presbyterian college in Salt Lake City. A series of donors approached the college to provide funds for building construction between 1895 and 1902, but these early arrangements did not come to fruition. Westminster College was officially founded in 1902 and funding for the first building, Converse Hall, soon followed. The Jacobethan-style building was designed by the prominent Salt Lake City firm of Ware & Treganza and built at a cost of $27,000. However, it remained unused until 1910, when additional funds were raised to complete the interior and furnish the building. By the time this photo was taken in 1912, the girls' dormitory, Ferry Hall, was built and allowed the institute to finally relocate to its new campus. At this time, the Westminster campus sat alone in an open field, largely accessed by dirt roads.

Approximately 2,000 undergraduate and 500 graduate students are enrolled at Westminster College today. Converse Hall remains the centerpiece of the campus and the focus of tremendous stewardship by the college. In the past, the historic structure has been adapted to serve the changing needs of the college, with roles ranging from a boys' dormitory and chemistry lab to a library, theater, and assembly hall. It now houses faculty offices and classrooms. Several of the other early buildings, such as Ferry Hall, have been demolished and replaced with new buildings, as the campus has been challenged with growth within a relatively confined geographic area. From its slow beginnings as an institute in the basement of the First Presbyterian Church, Westminster College has grown to be the largest private college in the state of Utah.

Utah's territorial prison was built in 1855 on a ten-acre plot in the far southeast section of what was known as the Big Field Survey. The site was eventually expanded to as much as 180 acres and included agricultural fields that served as productive rehabilitation for prisoners who worked to put fresh food on the prison's tables. The buildings included an adobe prison house, workshop, warden's house (seen in the center of this 1903 photo), and an adobe wall, twelve feet high and four feet thick, that enclosed seven acres. As adobe is mainly composed of dried mud, it's not surprising that it proved to be an inadequate deterrent to potential escapees. About a quarter of all prisoners escaped in the first twenty-five years of the prison's existence. The Utah State Penitentiary was demolished in 1951 when a new correctional facility was constructed at Point of the Mountain, approximately fifteen miles south.

The formation of Sugar House Park was considered as early as 1937 when the state legislature authorized investigating the cessation of operations on the prison site and its transfer to other parties. By 1951, the legislature concluded that the 120 acres that composed the site would be "perpetually used for public purposes." Salt Lake City and Salt Lake County agreed to buy the park from the state for $225,000. The Sugar House Park Authority was established in 1957 as a nonprofit organization to oversee park management, and they continue to manage it today. As the largest park in Salt Lake City, it is a destination for families, sports teams, runners, walkers, cyclists, and picnickers. Sugar House Park is linked by bike trails to the Jordan River Parkway and the Bonneville Shoreline Trail along the Wasatch Mountains (seen here) to the east.

Golf tournaments began in Salt Lake City's Gilmer Park area in 1898, which led to the area being called the Country Club. However, the first permanent home of the Salt Lake Country Club was at a nine-hole course in the Forest Dale neighborhood, where members built Utah's first golf clubhouse in 1906. The Mission-style building at this location, seen here in 1913, was the design of local architect Frederick Albert Hale, who kept company with the best golfers in the city at this time. Hale regularly beat everyone but was teased in newspaper cartoons for wearing boldly colored clothes. In 1920, the Salt Lake Country Club determined that its burgeoning membership deserved more than the current run of the links and signed a lease with the city for 268 acres farther east for a new location that would allow it to build a larger clubhouse and an eighteen-hole course.

Salt Lake Area Vocational School was started in 1948 and, after several name changes, became Salt Lake Community College (SLCC) in 1987. By 1990, SLCC had 10,000 students enrolled. SLCC acquired South High School from the school district in 1989, renovating and converting the facilities into their South City Campus. The renovation of the high school included upgrading the systems for college students and the addition of new common-use areas for a student union, cafeteria, and sports center. In 1992, South City Campus opened as a three-level complex that could serve more than 6,000 college students in 100 classrooms, labs, and student facilities. Its location in Salt Lake City boasts many activities that promote diversity, art, dance, and philosophy. South City Campus is also home to the Grand Theatre, which produces performing arts and humanities events for the community.

In 1893, Daniel Jackling and Robert Gemmell developed a profitable open-pit mining operation that became the Utah Copper Company (UCC) Mine. The rapid expansion of the UCC Mine after its founding in 1903 attracted the majority of good mining workers at the time, virtually stopping mining business in other parts of the state. Around 1920, the time of this photo, more than 20,000 people lived in towns and scattered camps throughout the canyons and hills of the Oquirrh Mountains that surrounded the mine. They built housing wherever they could find room, such as on the upper terraces of the open-pit mine. The smoother, lower terraces carried cars, trucks, and trains. Over time, the pit swallowed these areas and forced people and buildings to move, including entire towns. The last buildings in the towns of Highland Boy and Copperfield were gone by 1960, Bingham Canyon by 1972, and Lark by 1980, as the mine continued to expand.

The Kennecott Copper Company, founded in 1906 in Alaska, acquired a controlling interest in the Utah Copper Company in 1915. They subsequently built many state-of-the-art facilities for efficient processing. By World War II, Kennecott was called on to produce 30 percent of the copper used by the Allies, putting production at a world-record pace. The open-pit mine has been referred to as "the richest hole on earth," but two-thirds of the material removed is waste rock. Besides the main mineral of copper, silver, gold, and molybdenum are also extracted and refined. Rio Tinto Zinc Corporation purchased Kennecott in 1989 and has continued the company's expansion and modernization, making it one of most efficient copper producers in the world. At the mine's visitor center (see inset), the past and present come alive as one can see and touch mining equipment while overlooking the active excavation in the open pit. Today's open pit is one of the few man-made features on earth that can be seen from outer space.

Considered Utah's finest, most popular pleasure resort of its day, Saltair was a retreat from the disagreeable features of the city. Built by the LDS Church and opening in May 1893, Saltair provided a wholesome place of recreation for families and young people. It was to be the "Coney Island of the West." Richard K. A. Kletting, then considered Utah's foremost architect, designed the elaborate, whimsical pavilion on the lake. However, that first structure burned in 1925 and was replaced by this design by Ashton & Evans in 1926. Though the structure had been enlarged for bigger events, Saltair missed one season and never regained its former popularity.

Another fire destroyed the second building in 1970 after it was left abandoned for nearly ten years. In 1981, a modified version of Saltair was built near the site of the original, but it serves merely as a Byzantine-style reminder. Saltair once famously boasted the largest dance floor in the world. Through a series of recent owners, music has played an important part in keeping the crowds coming to the new Saltair and enjoying the Great Salt Lake. Rock concerts have generated large audiences in the new pavilion, far outnumbering adventurous Great Salt Lake swimmers. Where there was once more water, there is now more parking space.

Lake Park Resort, which opened in 1886, was one of the first resorts to open along the Great Salt Lake. Surrounding a central dancing pavilion were summer cottages, a merry-go-round, a roller-skating rink, a target-shooting range, and bowling alleys. Swimming in the lake was a prime summer activity. However, in 1893, the lake began to recede and left Lake Park one mile away from the water's edge. By 1896, Lake Park had moved farther inland and was renamed Lagoon after the small reservoir it used for activities. The Bamberger Railroad brought guests from Ogden and Salt Lake City to sample the first thrill rides in the park, like Shoot-the-Chutes, seen here on the left, but also for leisure activities such as rowing, as seen in this photo from 1907.

Lagoon's first major roller coaster was designed by renowned engineer John Miller and built in 1921. A fire in October 1953 burned several of the rides, along with a portion of the Miller-designed roller coaster. However, the fire gave the owners a chance to redesign the park, offering accessibility to the new highway and extended thrill rides. Legends of rock and roll, including the Doors, the Rolling Stones, and Jimi Hendrix, played at Lagoon after the Patio Gardens entertainment venue was constructed in 1954. While the historic roller coaster continues to faithfully run for its fans young and old, new rides that attempt great gravity-defying loops seem to be the most popular attraction today.

In 1871, farmer William Stuart Brighton built a cabin on eighty acres at the top of Big Cottonwood Canyon. Miners moving between Alta and Park City stopped here to rest and eat, as the Brighton cabin was a convenient halfway point with excellent food and pristine alpine views. Encouraged by this passing trade, the first Brighton Hotel was built in 1874 as a two-story wood structure with seven small bedrooms, a dining room, and a lean-to kitchen. Eventually, several one- and two-room cabins were built for vacationing families. Each cabin had a wood-burning stove, and lighting was provided by a kerosene lamp or candle crafted from a lard bucket or large tomato can. As more people sought escape from the summer's heat in the Salt Lake Valley, the Brightons built a three-story hotel of rustic design in 1893. The hotel was demolished in 1945.